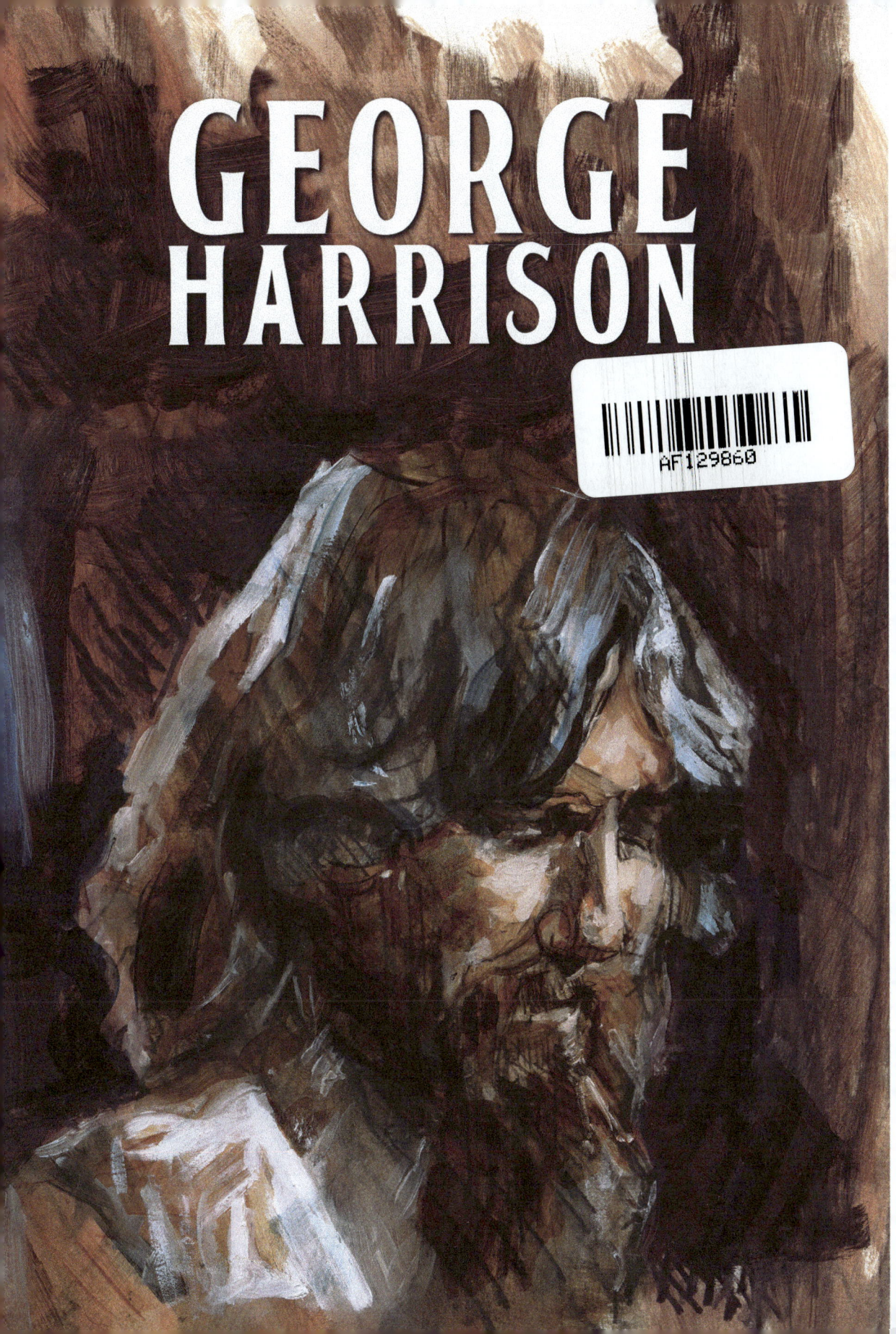

WITH THE AID OF FRIENDS LIKE RINGO, DAVE MASON, ALAN WHITE, MAL EVANS, BADFINGER, DEREK AND THE DOMINOES, KLAUS VOORMAN, BILLY PRESTON, AND BOB DYLAN, WHOM I ADMIRE, I FINALLY FINISHED A MASTERPIECE. *A TRIPLE ALBUM* HIT NUMBER ONE IN THE US AND THE UK.

THE FIRST SINGLE, *"MY SWEET LORD,"* IS RELEASED ON NOVEMBER 28, 1970.

ON NOVEMBER 10, 1971, BRIGHT TUNES SUES ME, STATING I PLAGIARIZED THAT SONG. *ME!*

THE TRIAL DRUG ON FOR TWENTY YEARS, FINALLY ENDING IN FAVOR OF THE PLAINTIFFS ON NOVEMBER 5, 1990. THE VERDICT DECLARED I'D UNCONSCIOUSLY PLAGIARIZED THEIR WORK.

GOING TO COURT WAS A PAIN IN THE ASS. I'M WILLING TO BET THAT EACH TIME I WRITE A SONG, THERE'LL BE SOMEONE TO TELL ME HE ALREADY WROTE THAT NOTE, THAT RIFF, THAT CHORD, THAT LYRIC. PLAGIARISM INDEED.

STILL, RAVI MOTIVATED ME TO CONTINUE MY WORK. I RAISED MONEY IN SUPPORT OF *BANGLADESH*, WHICH WAS RAVAGED BY FAMINE AND CIVIL WAR.

THE SINGLE, "BANGLA DESH," WITH "DEEP BLUE" AS THE B SIDE, WAS A FIRST STEP. BUT IT WASN'T ENOUGH. I HAD TO CALL UPON MY FRIENDS IF I WAS GOING TO SEE REAL CHANGE.

AS I'VE GROWN OLDER, I FEEL LIKE I'VE FOUND MY *PLACE*. I CAN SEE THINGS MORE CLEARLY THAN EVER.

FOLLOWING ROY'S DEATH, THE YEARS WOULD PASS QUICKLY, FULL OF PROJECTS WITH RINGO, DOCUMENTARIES, ALBUM COMPILATIONS, AND NEWLY-DISCOVERED RECORDINGS THAT QUICKLY BROUGHT THE BEATLES NAME BACK INTO PUBLIC CONSCIOUSNESS. ALL THE WHILE, I STRUGGLED TO SEEK BALANCE BETWEEN INNER PEACE AND ANGER.

LIKE MOST THINGS, *POPULARITY* IS FLEETING AND *PEACE* IS DIFFICULT TO ACHIEVE, LET ALONE MAINTAIN.

I ADMIRED FORMULA 1 DRIVER *AYRTON SENNA*, ONLY TO LEARN OF HIS DEATH AFTER CRASHING HIS CAR INTO A WALL.

HE WAS DRIVING OVER 186 MILES PER HOUR.

I WAS...DEVASTATED.

IS IT ANY WONDER THAT I TURNED AGAIN TO *RAVI SHANKAR*, MY SURROGATE FATHER?

IF YOU HAVEN'T EXPERIENCED THIS FORM OF *ACCEPTANCE*, A POWERFUL FEELING I CAN'T EXPLAIN, I AM TRULY SAD FOR YOU. HE URGED ME TO AGAIN EXPLORE THE DEPTHS OF MY CREATIVITY, BUT I AM AGAIN DRAWN TO THE PEACE THAT ACCOMPANIES ISOLATION...

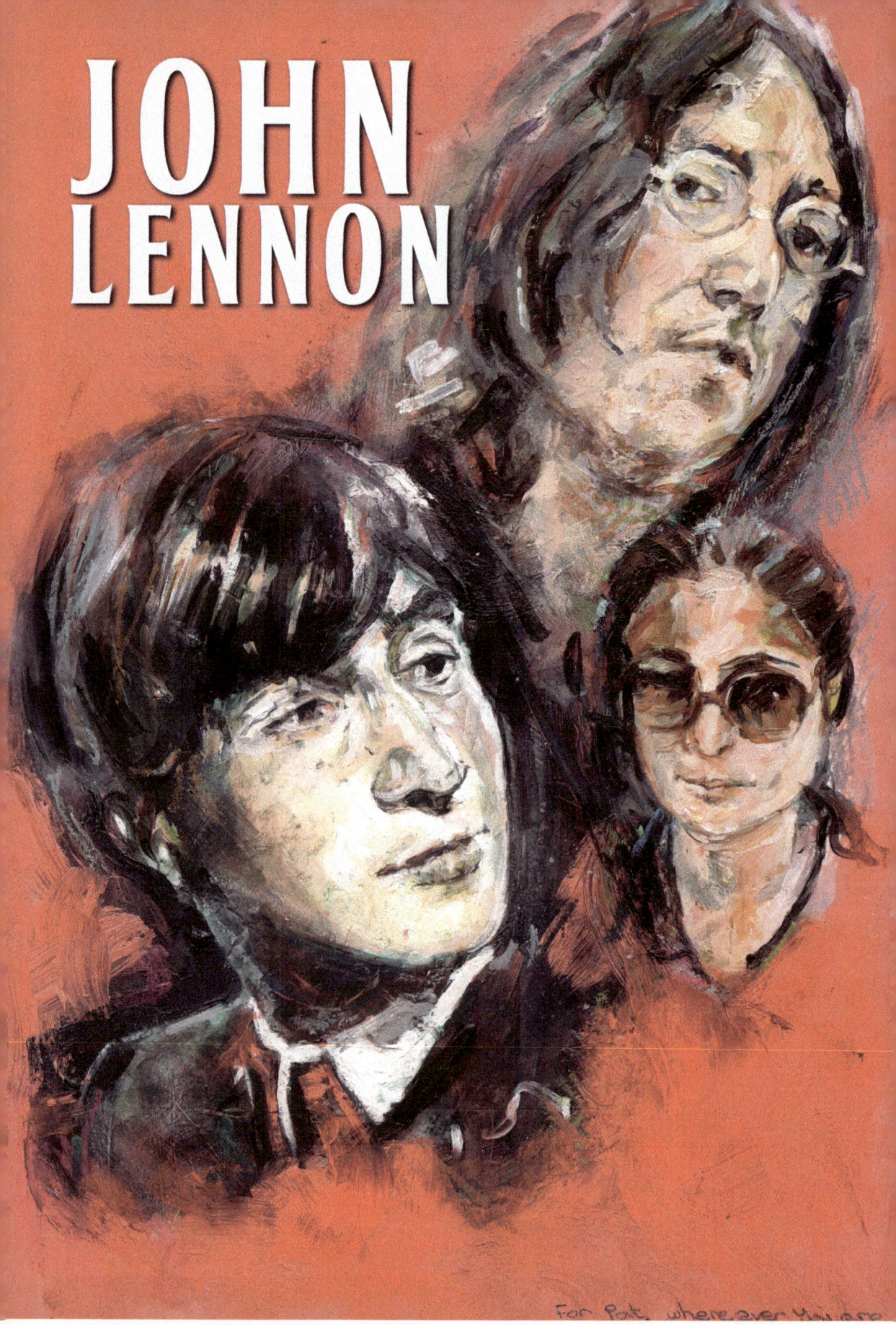

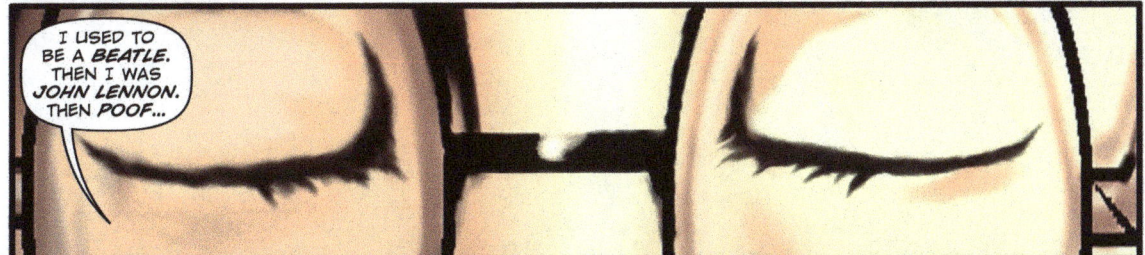

The Beatles played their last live performance on January 30th, 1969 on the roof of the Apple Corp. building.

By that time, Lennon, inspired by his muse, Yoko Ono, was already forging his own musical identity.

In short order, he recorded the avante-garde albums Two Virgins, Life With The Lions and Wedding Album.

A loose group of musicians dubbed The Plastic Ono Band released Live Peace in Toronto in 1969.

...*New York City*, where creativity crackled like lightning and revolution was in the air.

John was champing at the bit to be a *part* of it all.

John And Yoko released the song Happy Xmas (War Is Over)

John paid for 12 massive billboards displayed across the US to further emphasize their anti war sentiments!

Lennon continued to embrace the injustices of the world with the album *Sometime In New York City* which addressed racial issues, the war in Northern Ireland and women as second class citizens with the controversial song *Woman Is The Nigger of The World*.

By 1973, John and Yoko's relationship began to unravel amid tensions both personal and professional.

During the recording of the album **Mind Games**...

...John and Yoko separated.

John Lennon was on his own. His *lost weekend* had begun.

And there were *two sides* to this story.

Lennon's 1974 album, **Walls and Bridges**, produced his only number one hit, **Whatever Gets You Through The Night**.

John and Yoko finally worked through their problems and were back together in January of 1975.

Yoko became pregnant shortly thereafter.

Lennon's second son, **Sean**, was born in October of that year.

John was so caught up in the idea of **family** and **fatherhood** that he abruptly withdrew from music and became a **house husband**.

He would regularly get up at 6am to make Sean's breakfast...

...or get down on the floor to play games or sing songs to his young son.

Lennon fulfilled his record company contract with his greatest hits collection, **Shaved Fish**.

Now he was truly **free**.

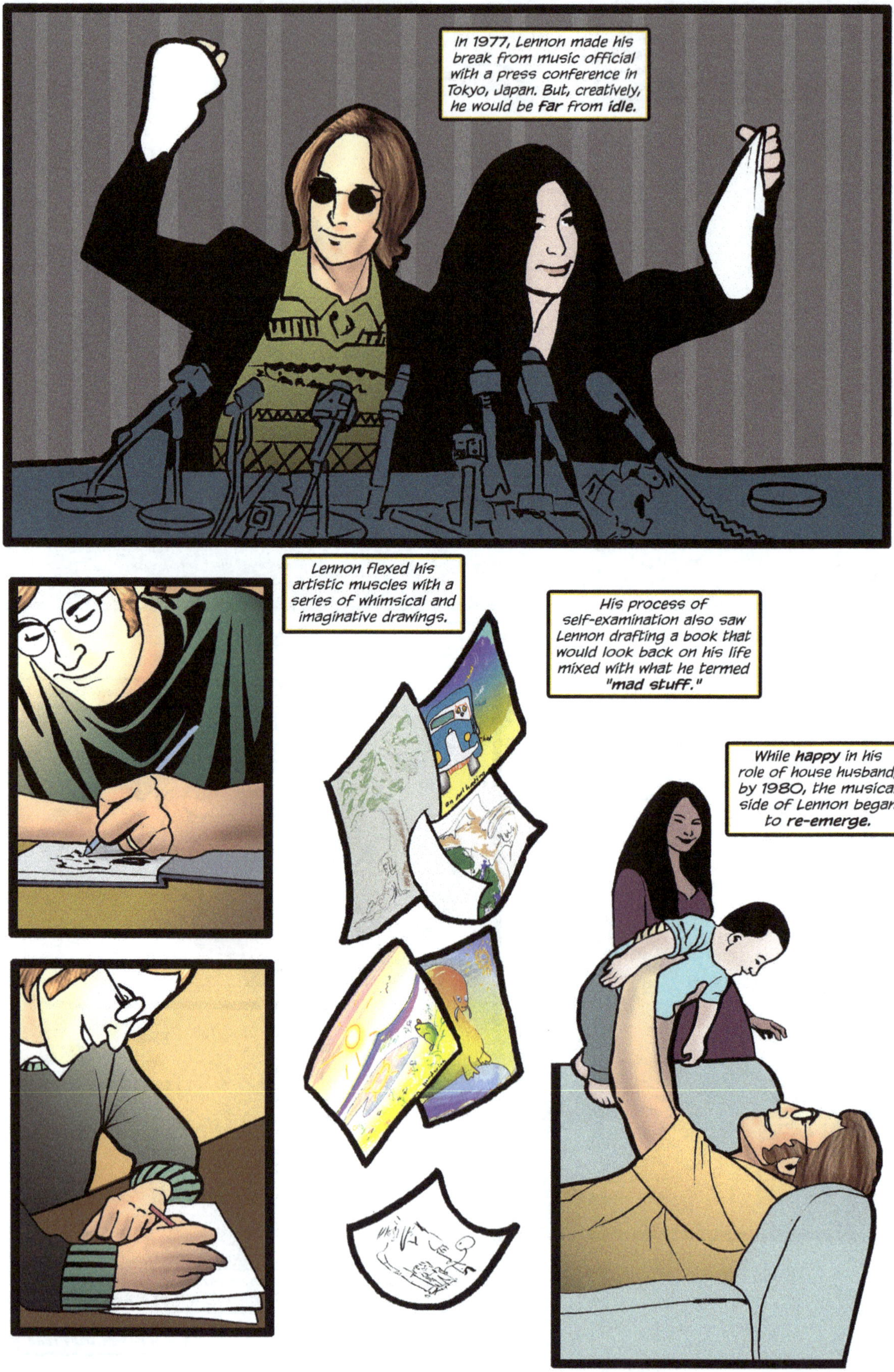

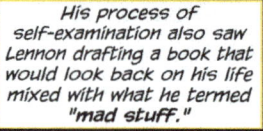

In 1977, Lennon made his break from music official with a press conference in Tokyo, Japan. But, creatively, he would be far from idle.

Lennon flexed his artistic muscles with a series of whimsical and imaginative drawings.

His process of self-examination also saw Lennon drafting a book that would look back on his life mixed with what he termed "mad stuff."

While happy in his role of house husband, by 1980, the musical side of Lennon began to re-emerge.

At approximately 10:50pm, Lennon and Yoko were about to enter their apartment building, *The Dakota*, when...

....Mark David Chapman fired four bullets into John Lennon's **back**.

Lennon was rushed to nearby Roosevelt Hospital where he was pronounced dead at 11:07pm.

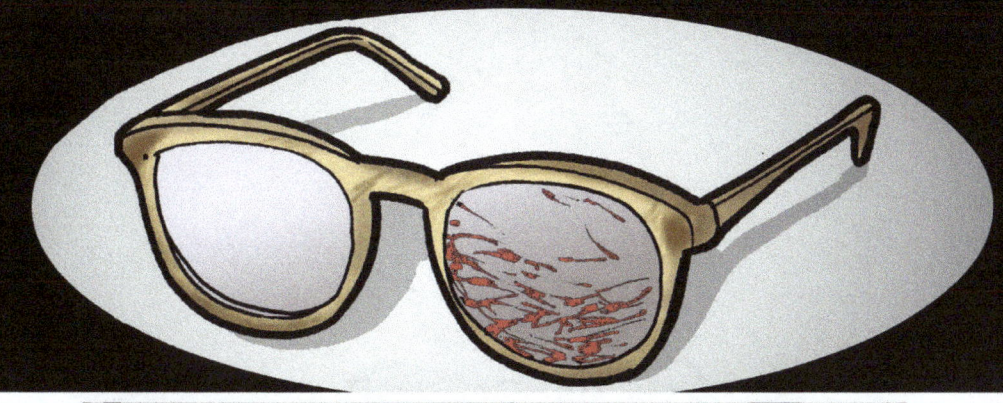

Lennon's body was *cremated* at Ferncliff Cemetery in Hartsdale, New York.

His ashes were scattered in New York's Central Park.

Lennon's earthly journey was over.

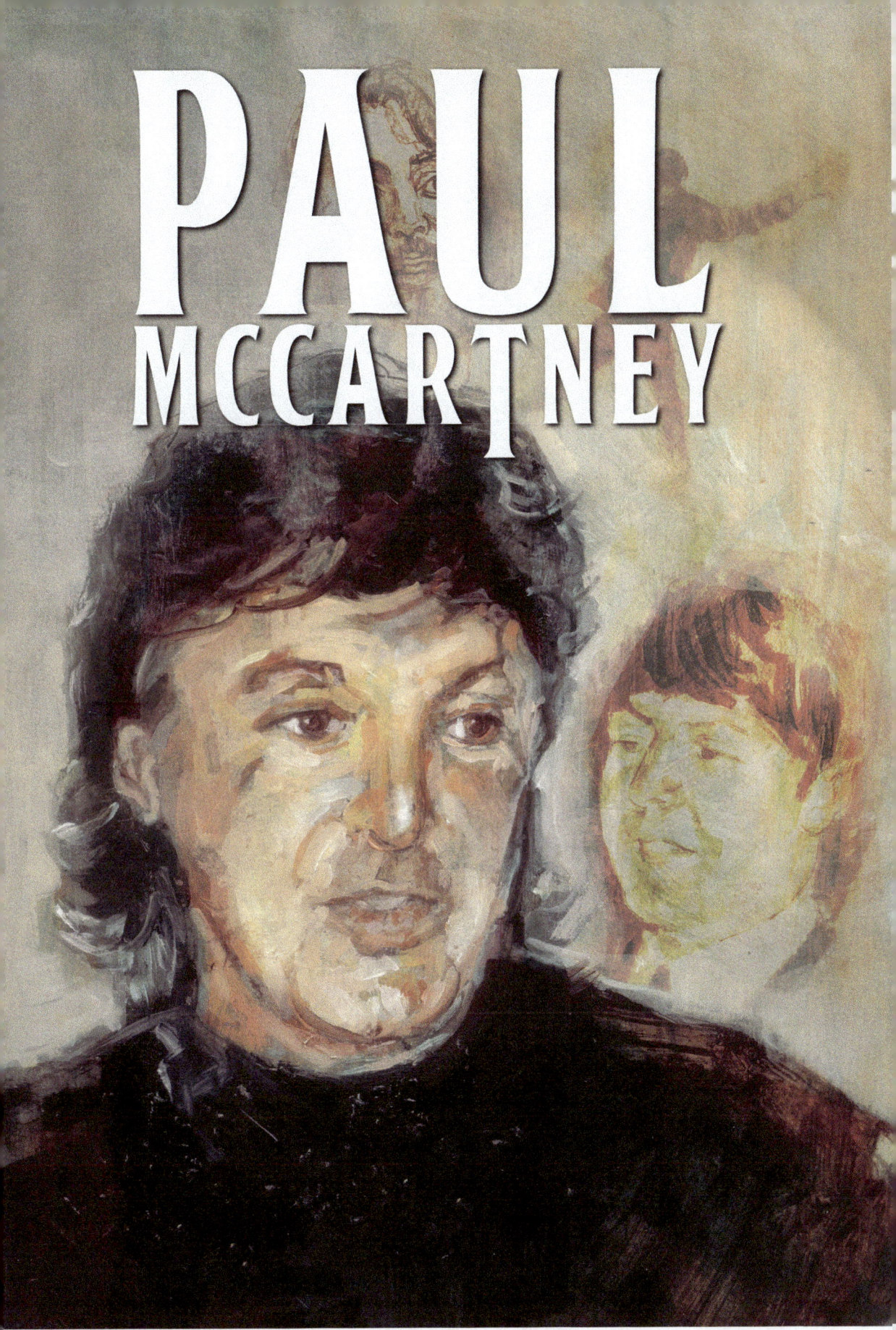

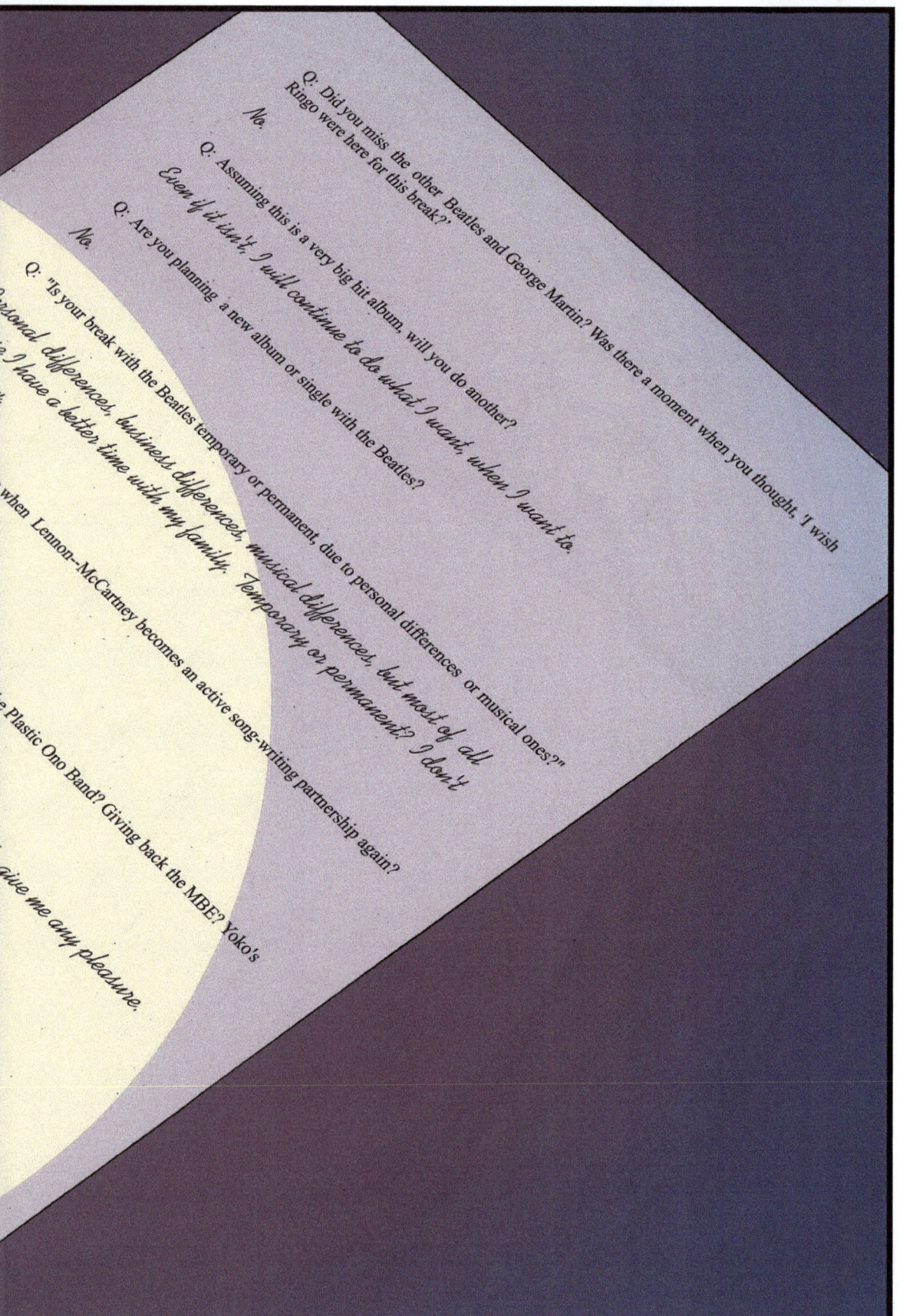

Q: Did you miss the other Beatles and George Martin? Was there a moment when you thought, I wish Ringo were here for this break?

No.

Q: Assuming this is a very big hit album, will you do another?

Even if it isn't, I will continue to do what I want, when I want to.

Q: Are you planning a new album or single with the Beatles?

No.

Q: "Is your break with the Beatles temporary or permanent, due to personal differences or musical ones?"

Personal differences, business differences, musical differences, but most of all because I have a better time with my family. Temporary or permanent? I don't know.

Q: ...when Lennon–McCartney becomes an active song-writing partnership again?

...

Q: ...the Plastic Ono Band? Giving back the MBE? Yoko's ...

...give me any pleasure.

STRICTLY SPEAKING SHE HARMONIZES, BUT OF COURSE IT'S MORE THAN THAT.

SHE'S A SHOULDER TO LEAN ON, A SECOND OPINION, AND A PHOTOGRAPHER OF RENOWN.

MORE THAN ALL THIS.

SHE BELIEVES IN ME.

CONSTANTLY.

THE END

WHO WANTS TO PLAY THE DRUM?

MUSIC

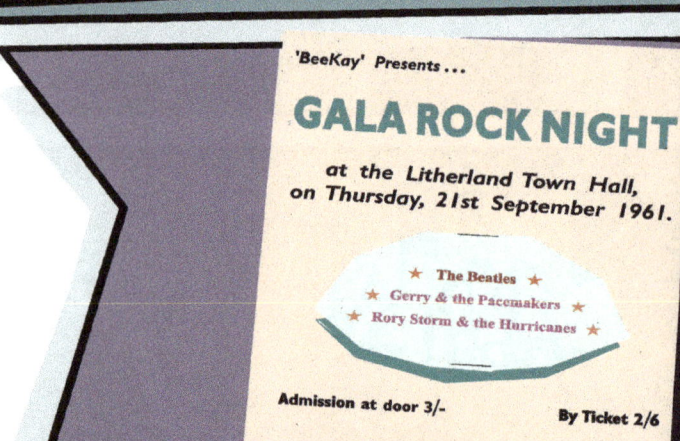

CAN I GET AN AUTOGRAPH?

I BET YOU WON'T GO AND KISS PAUL.
JUST BECAUSE YOU'RE SCARED TO DO IT.
YOU'RE SCARED, MAUREEN!
OKAY, FINE.

SO, DO YOU WANNA DANCE?

Writer: Carlos Pagola Morales, Marc Shapiro, Richard Elms, David Cromarty

Art: Angel Bernuy, Luciano Kars, Orlando Maro, Victor Moura

Letters: Benjamin Glibert, Warren Montgomery

Colors: Victor Moura, Luciano Kars, Orlando Maro

Cover: George Amaru

Bonus Images: Graham Hill

Darren G. Davis — Publisher
Maggie Jessup — Publicity
Susan Ferris — Entertainment Manager
Steven Diggs Jr. — Marketing Manager

ORBIT: BEATLES GRAPHIC NOVEL AND CONTENTS ARE COPYRIGHT © AND ™ DARREN G. DAVIS. ALL RIGHTS RESERVED. TIDALWAVE IS COPYRIGHT © AND ™ DARREN G. DAVIS. ALL RIGHTS RESERVED. ANY REPRODUCTION OF THIS MATERIAL IS STRICTLY PROHIBITED IN ANY MEDIA FORM OTHER THAN FOR PROMOTIONAL PURPOSES UNLESS DARREN G. DAVIS OR TIDALWAVE PUBLISHING GIVES WRITTEN CONSENT. PRINTED IN THE USA www.tidalwavecomics.com

Lightning Source UK Ltd.
Milton Keynes UK
UKHW050008170123
415286UK00007B/54